EASY GUITAR
WITH NOTES & TAB

Best of UNITED

2   STRUM AND PICK PATTERNS

6   ALL I NEED IS YOU

3   CAME TO MY RESCUE

10   EVERYDAY

18   FIRE FALL DOWN

13   FROM THE INSIDE OUT

22   GOD IS GREAT

28   HOSANNA

32   KING OF MAJESTY

25   LEAD ME TO THE CROSS

34   ONE WAY

40   SALVATION IS HERE

44   SAVIOUR KING

37   SHOUT UNTO GOD

48   THE STAND

50   TAKE IT ALL

60   TELL THE WORLD

54   TIL I SEE YOU

56   THE TIME HAS COME

ISBN 978-1-4234-9911-4

7777 W. BLUEMOUND RD. P.O. BOX 13819 MILWAUKEE, WI 53213

Visit Hal Leonard Online at
www.halleonard.com

STRUM AND PICK PATTERNS

This chart contains the suggested strum and pick patterns that are referred to by number at the beginning of each song in this book. The symbols ⊓ and ∨ in the strum patterns refer to down and up strokes, respectively. The letters in the pick patterns indicate which right-hand fingers play which strings.

p = thumb
i = index finger
m = middle finger
a = ring finger

For example; Pick Pattern 2
is played: thumb - index - middle - ring

Strum Patterns

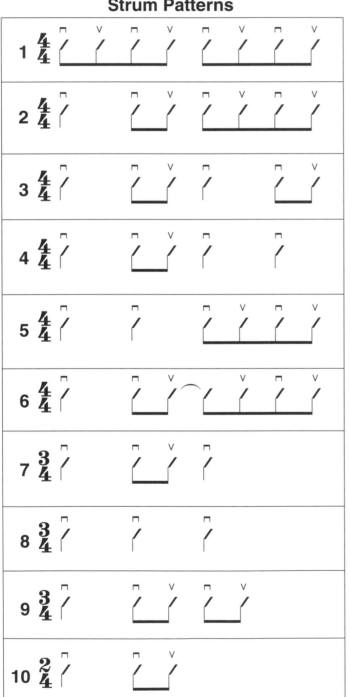

Pick Patterns

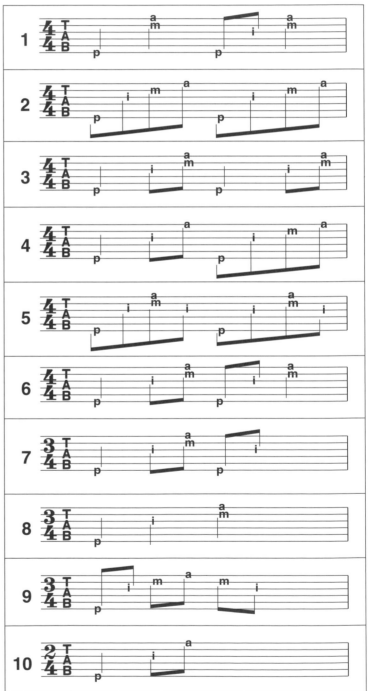

You can use the 3/4 Strum and Pick Patterns in songs written in compound meter (6/8, 9/8, 12/8, etc.).
For example, you can accompany a song in 6/8 by playing the 3/4 pattern twice in each measure.
The 4/4 Strum and Pick Patterns can be used for songs written in cut time (¢) by doubling the note
time values in the patterns. Each pattern would therefore last two measures in cut time.

Came to My Rescue

Words and Music by Marty Sampson, Dylan Thomas and Joel Davies

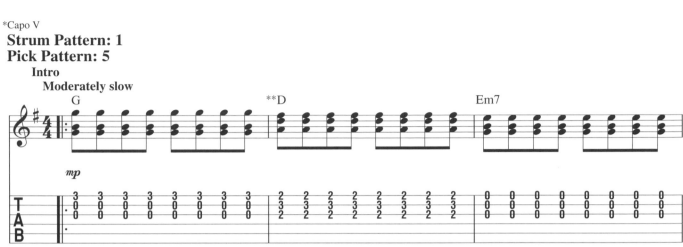

*Capo V

Strum Pattern: 1
Pick Pattern: 5

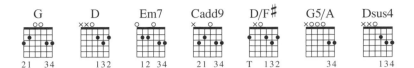

*Optional: To match recording, place capo at 5th fret.   **2nd time, substitute D/F#

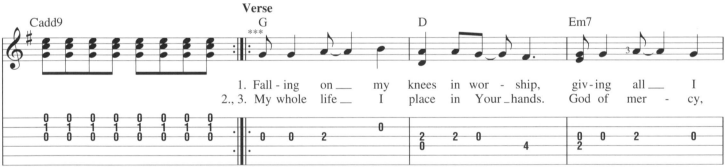

***1st & 2nd times, sung one octave lower.

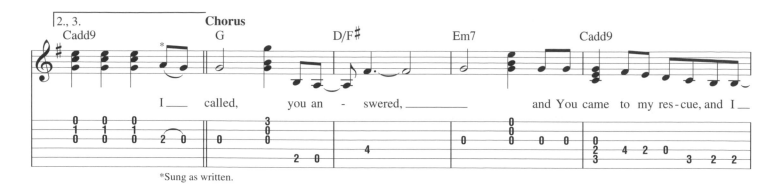

*Sung as written.

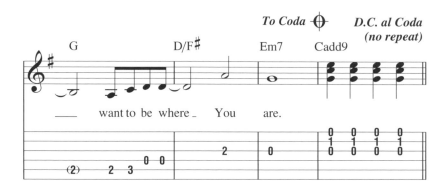

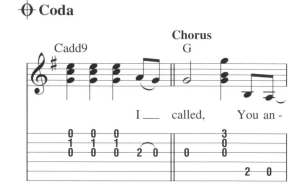

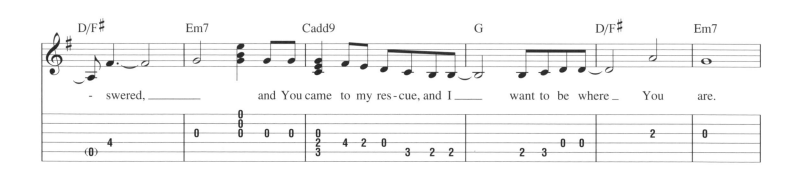

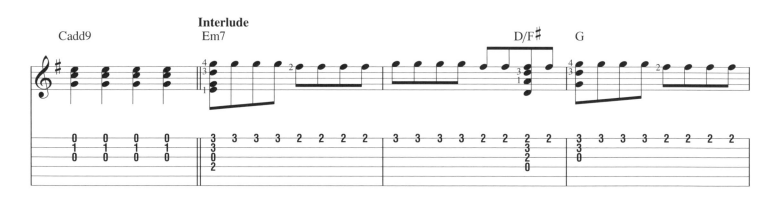

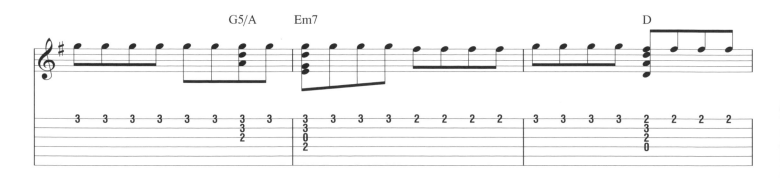

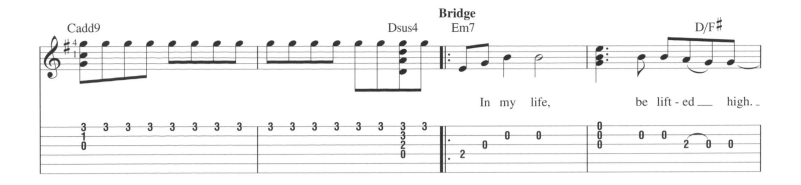

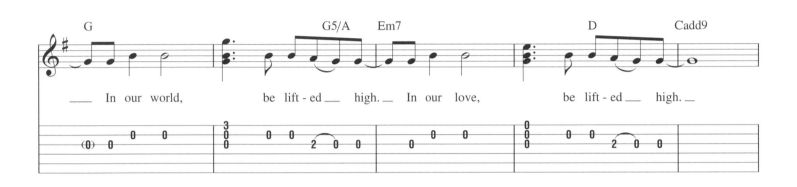

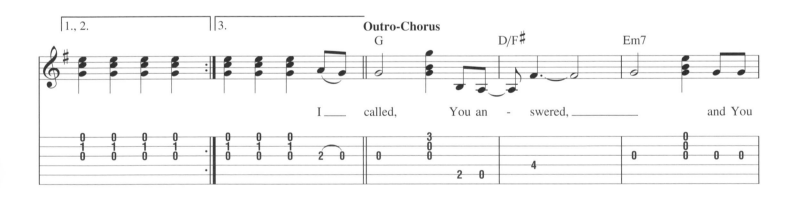

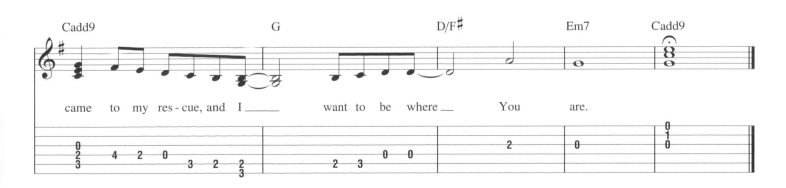

All I Need Is You

Words and Music by Marty Sampson

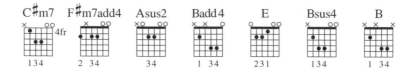

Strum Pattern: 3
Pick Pattern: 3

Intro

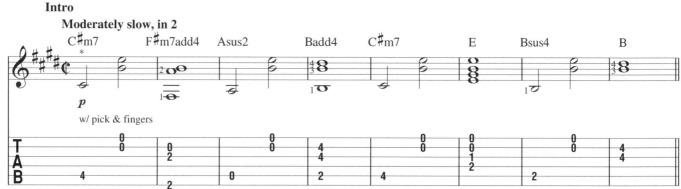

*Kybd. arr. for gtr., next 8 meas.

Verse

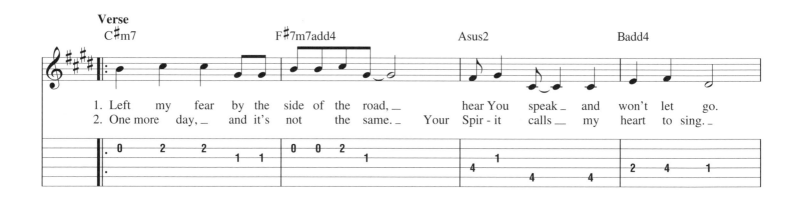

1. Left my fear by the side of the road, __ hear You speak __ and won't let go.
2. One more day, __ and it's not the same. __ Your Spir-it calls __ my heart to sing. __

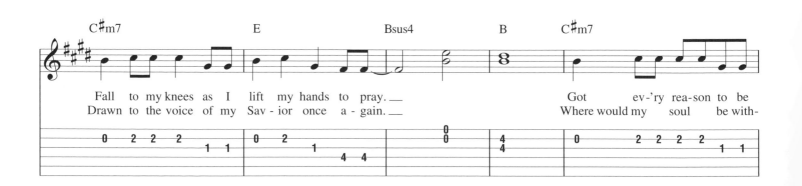

Fall to my knees as I lift my hands to pray. __ Got ev-'ry rea-son to be
Drawn to the voice of my Sav-ior once a-gain. __ Where would my soul be with-

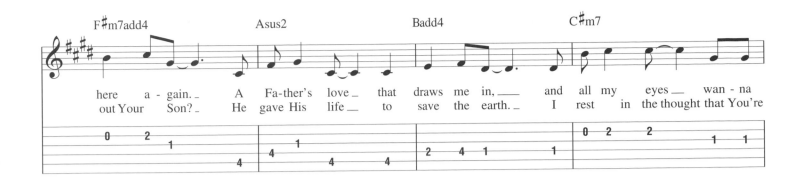

here a - gain._ A Fa-ther's love _ that draws me in, __ and all my eyes _ wan - na
out Your Son? _ He gave His life _ to save the earth. _ I rest in the thought that You're

%̖ Chorus

see is a glimpse of You. __} All I need is You. All I need is
watch-ing o - ver me. __}

You, _ Lord, ___ is You, _ Lord. All I need is You.

To Coda 1 ⊕   *To Coda 2* ⊕ |1. |2.   *D.S. al Coda 1*

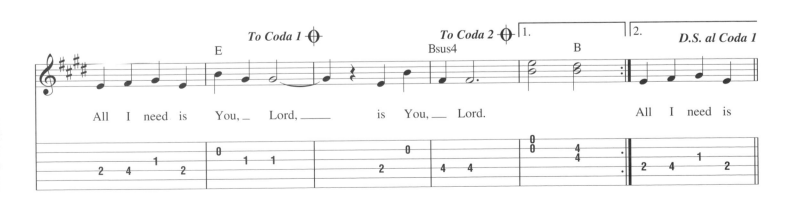

All I need is You, _ Lord, ___ is You, _ Lord.   All I need is

⊕ Coda 1

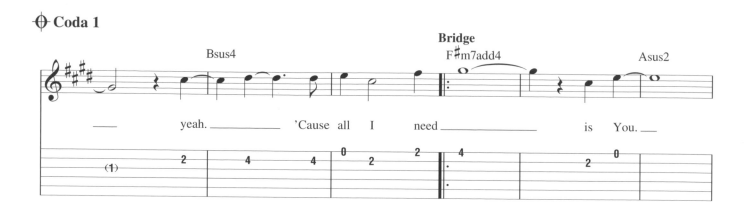

yeah. _____ 'Cause all I need _____ is You. __

All I need _____ is You. __ 'Cause all I need _ __ is You. __

⊕ Coda 2

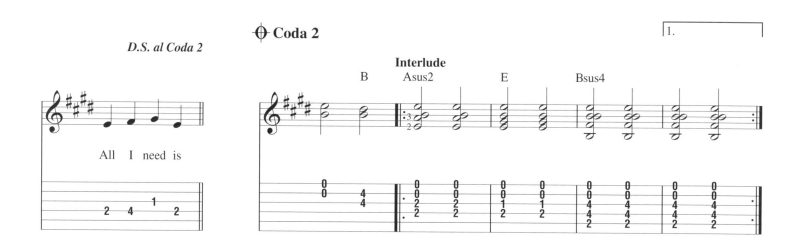

D.S. al Coda 2

All I need is

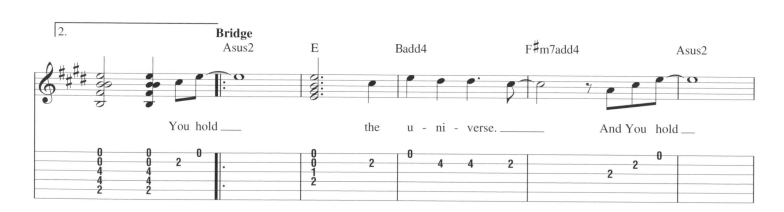

You hold ___ the u - ni - verse. _____ And You hold __

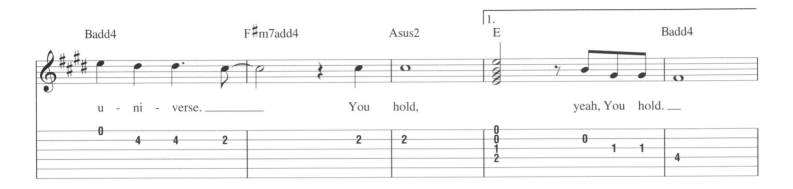

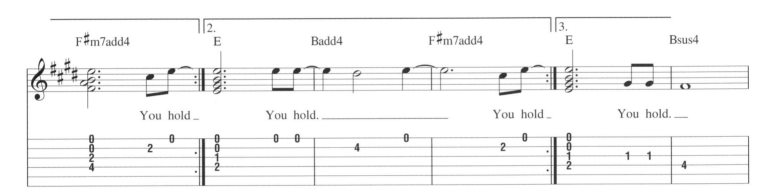

Outro-Chorus

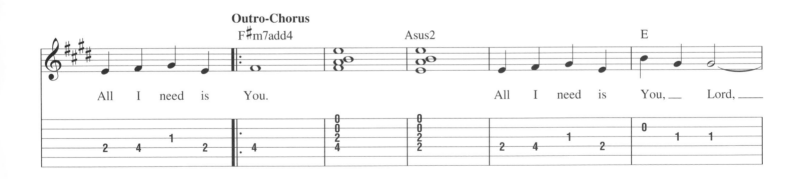

Everyday

Words and Music by Joel Houston

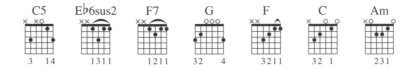

Strum Pattern: 2
Pick Pattern: 2

Intro

Moderately fast

𝄋 Verse

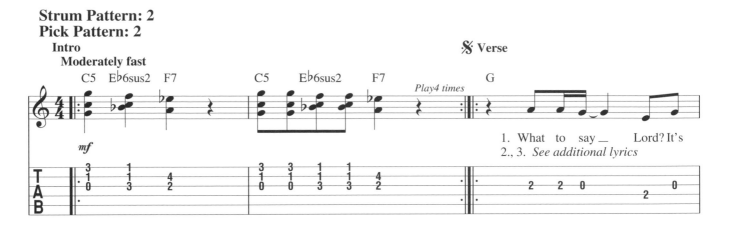

1. What to say _ Lord? It's
2., 3. *See additional lyrics*

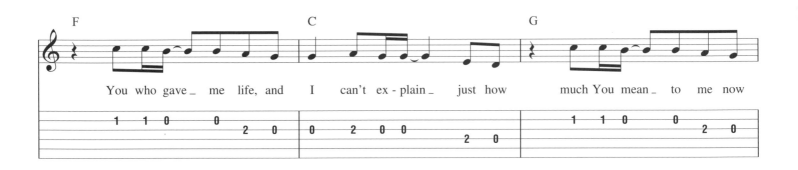

You who gave _ me life, and I can't ex-plain _ just how much You mean _ to me now

that You have saved _ me, Lord. I give all that _ I am to You, that ev-'ry day _ I can

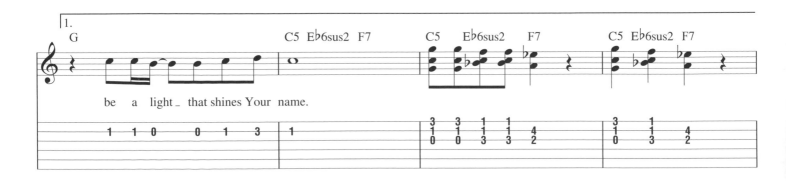

be a light _ that shines Your name.

© 1999 HILLSONG PUBLISHING (ASCAP)
Admin. in the United States and Canada at EMICMGPUBLISHING.COM

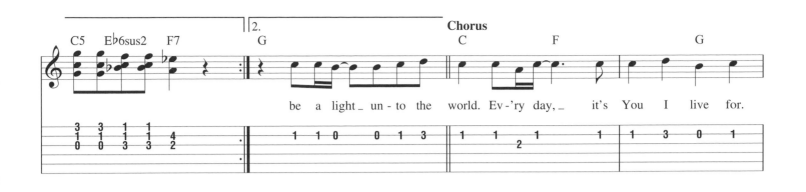

be a light _ un-to the world. Ev-'ry day, _ it's You I live for.

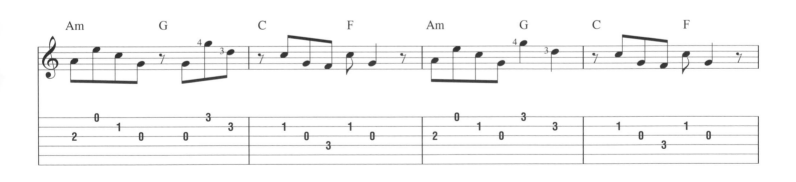

Ev-'ry day, _ I'll fol-low af-ter You. Ev-'ry day, _ I'll walk with You, my Lord.

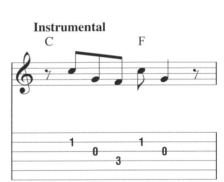

Coda

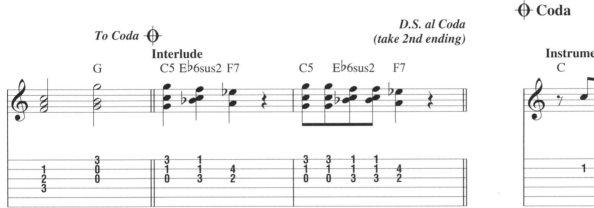

To Coda

D.S. al Coda
(take 2nd ending)

Interlude

Instrumental

It's

Bridge

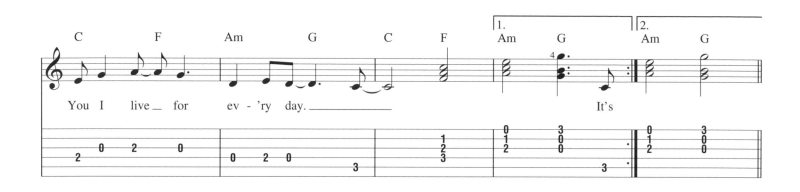

Outro-Chorus

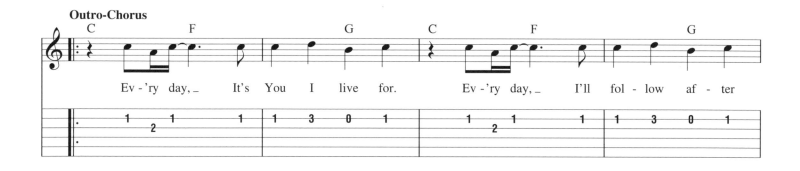

Additional Lyrics

2., 3. Ev'ry day, Lord, I learn to stand up on Your Word,
And I pray that I, I might come to know You more,
That You would guide me in ev'ry single step I take.
That ev'ry day I can be a light unto the world.

From the Inside Out

Words and Music by Joel Houston

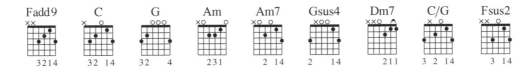

Strum Pattern: 2, 3
Pick Pattern: 5

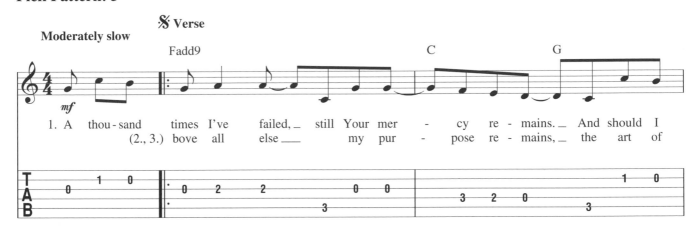

1. A thou-sand times I've failed, _ still Your mer - cy re - mains. _ And should I
(2., 3.) bove all else _ my pur - pose re - mains, _ the art of

stum - ble a - gain, _ I'm caught _ in Your grace.
los - ing my - self _ in bring - ing You praise. } Ev - er - last -

Chorus

- ing, Your light will shine when all else fades. Nev - er - end -

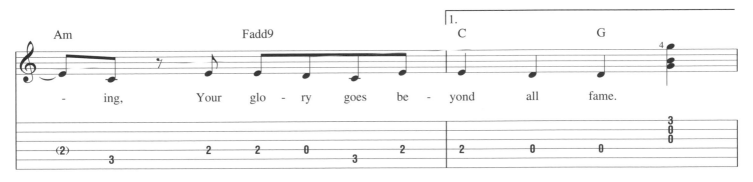

- ing, Your glo - ry goes be - yond all fame.

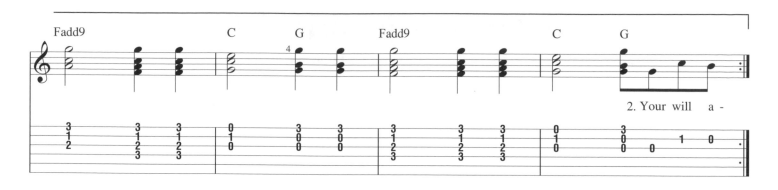

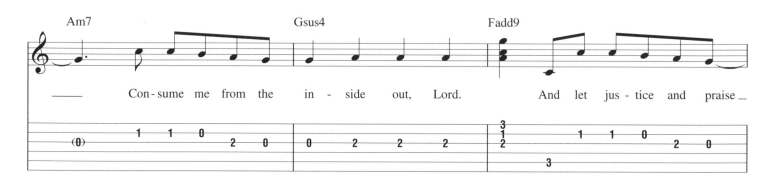

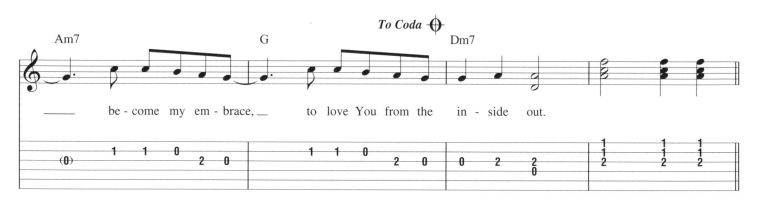

D.S. al Coda
(take 2nd ending)

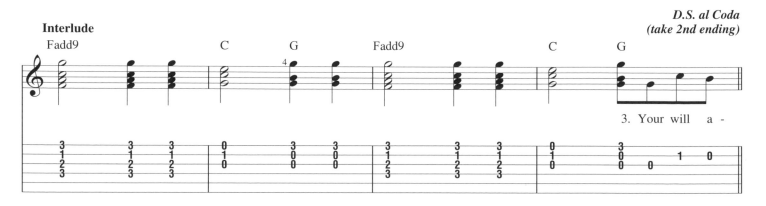

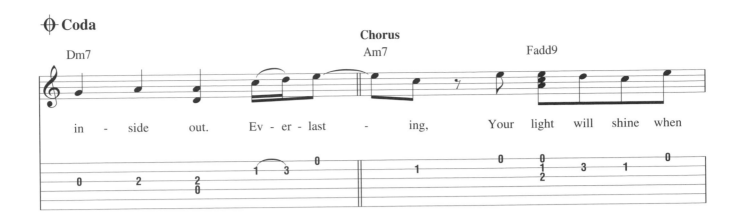

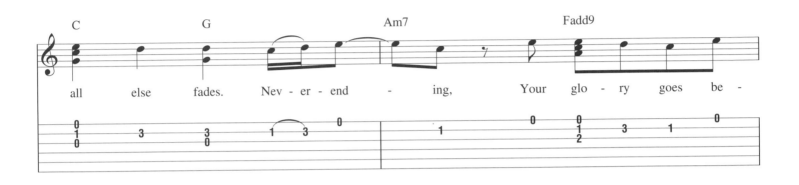

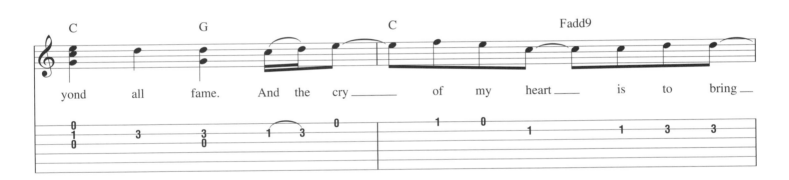

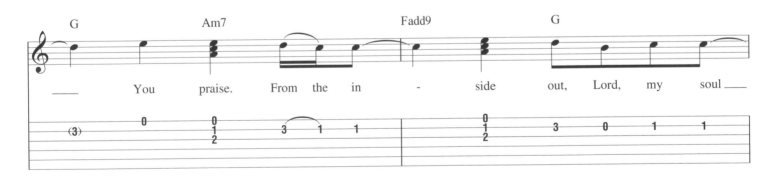

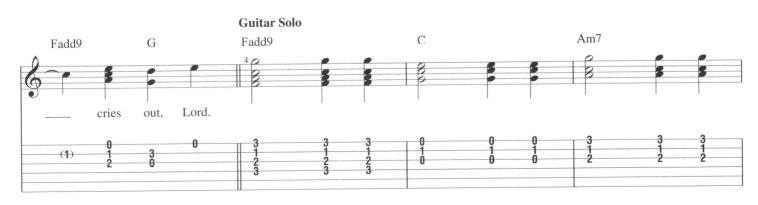

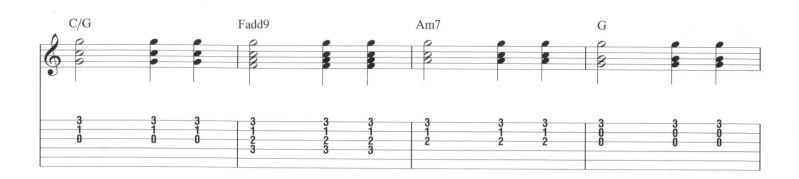

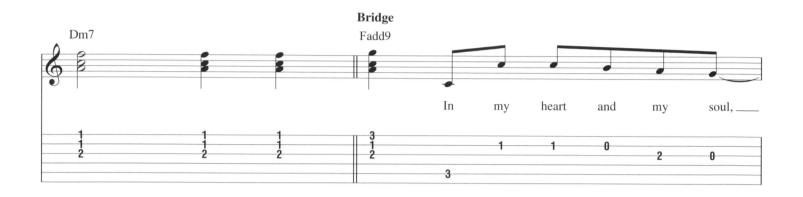

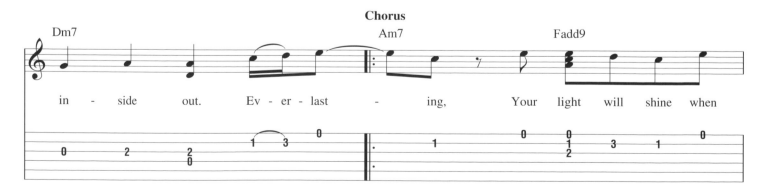

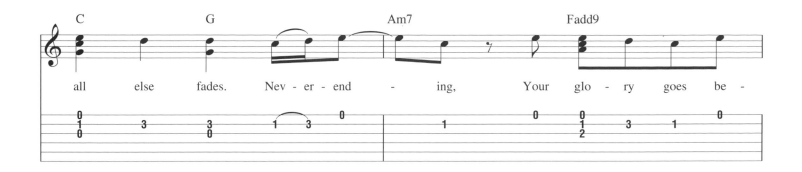

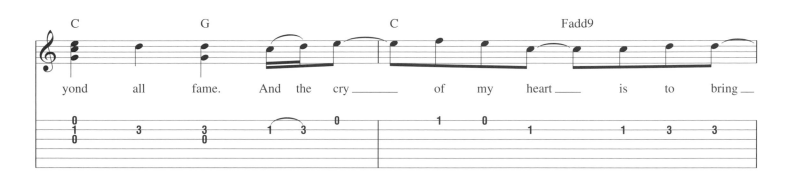

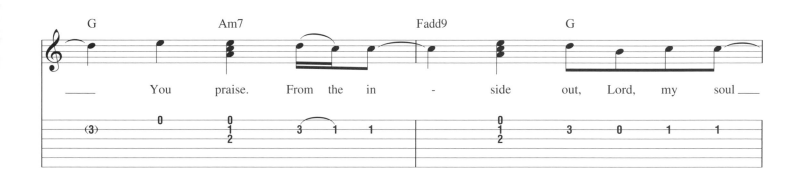

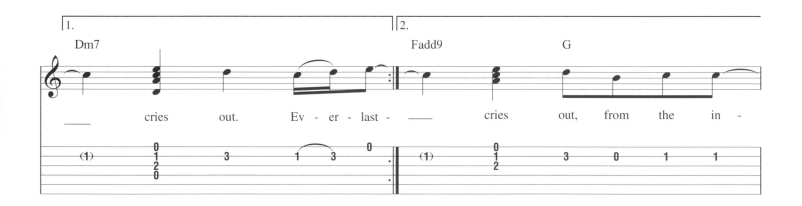

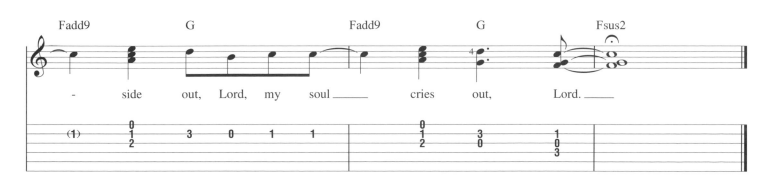

Fire Fall Down

Words and Music by Matt Crocker

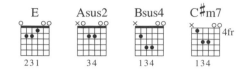

*Capo II

Strum Pattern: 2
Pick Pattern: 4

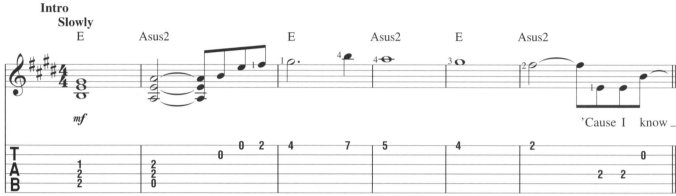

*Optional: To match recording, place capo at 2nd fret.

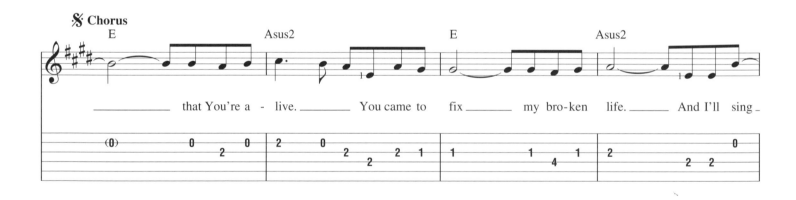

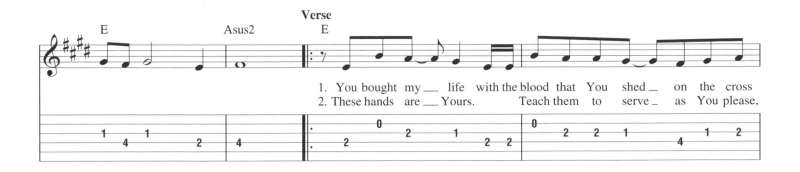

Verse

1. You bought my ___ life with the blood that You shed ___ on the cross
2. These hands are ___ Yours. Teach them to serve ___ as You please,

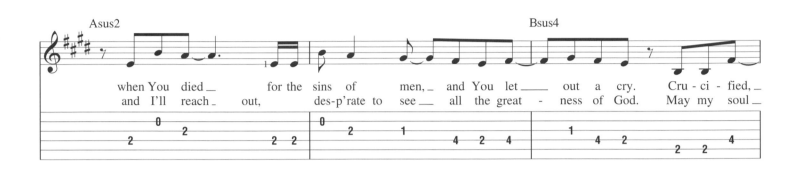

when You died ___ for the sins of men, ___ and You let ___ out a cry. Cru - ci - fied, ___
and I'll reach ___ out, des-p'rate to see ___ all the great - ness of God. May my soul ___

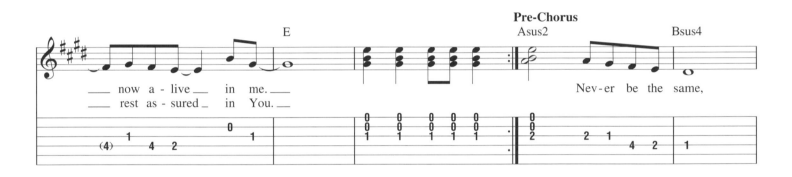

___ now a - live ___ in me. ___
___ rest as - sured ___ in You. ___

Pre-Chorus

Nev - er be the same,

D.S. al Coda

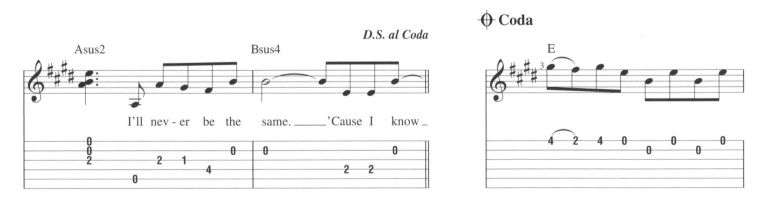

I'll nev - er be the same. ___ 'Cause I know ___

Coda

Verse

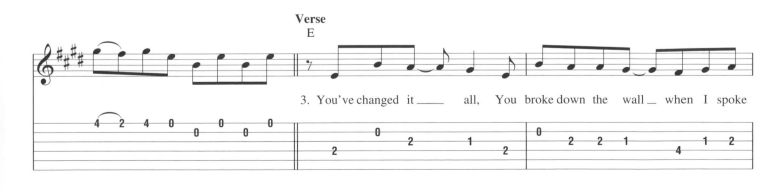

3. You've changed it ___ all, You broke down the wall ___ when I spoke

and con-fessed. ___ In You, I am blessed. Now I walk ___ in the light, in vic-to-

- ri-ous sight ___ of You. ___   Nev-er be the same,

Pre-Chorus

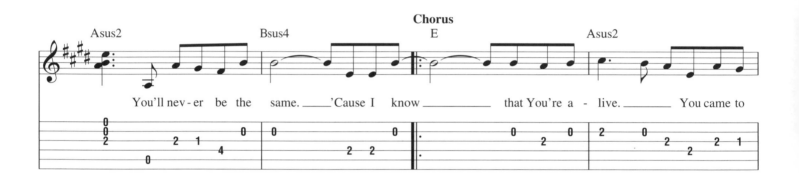

Chorus

You'll nev-er be the same. ___'Cause I know _____ that You're a-live. _____ You came to

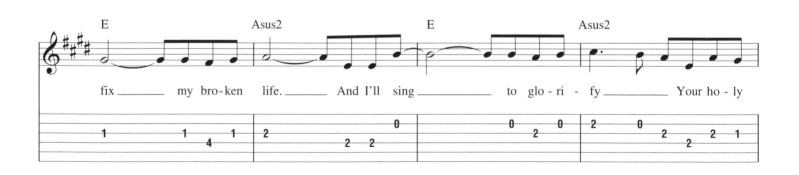

fix _____ my bro-ken life. _____ And I'll sing _____ to glo-ri-fy _____ Your ho-ly

Interlude

name, Je-sus ___ Christ. ___'Cause I know _ ____Christ. ___

Outro

Your fire _____ fall down, Your fire _____ fall down _ on us _ we pray. _ As we

Play 7 times

seek. Your fire _____ fall down, Your fire _____ fall down _ on us _ we pray. _ As we

seek. Show me _ Your heart, show me _ Your way, show me _ Your glo - ry.

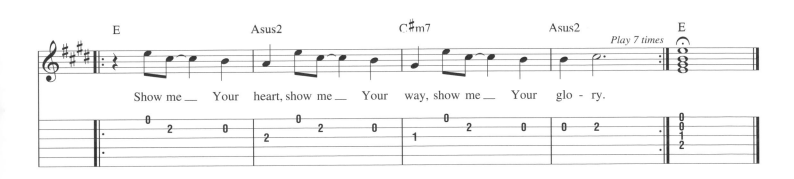

Play 7 times

Show me _ Your heart, show me _ Your way, show me _ Your glo - ry.

God Is Great

Words and Music by Marty Sampson

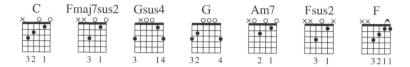

C   Fmaj7sus2   Gsus4   G   Am7   Fsus2   F

*Tune down 1/2 step:
(low to high) E♭-A♭-D♭-G♭-B♭-E♭

Strum Pattern: 5
Pick Pattern: 5

Verse
Fast

*Optional: To match recording, tune down 1/2 step.

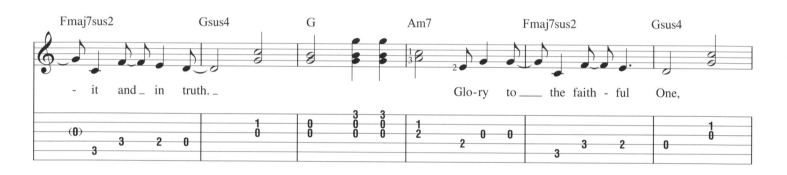

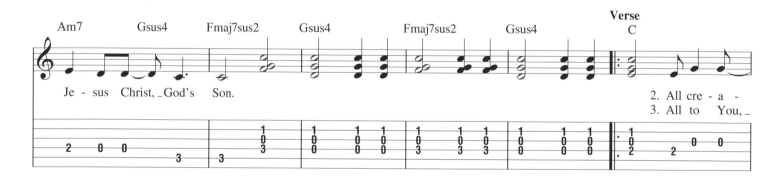

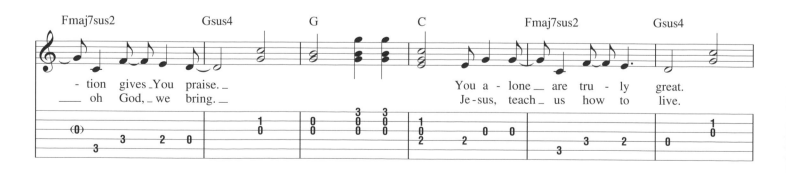

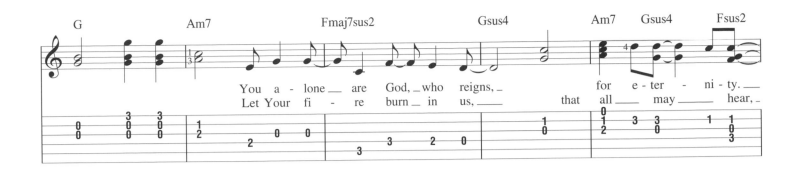

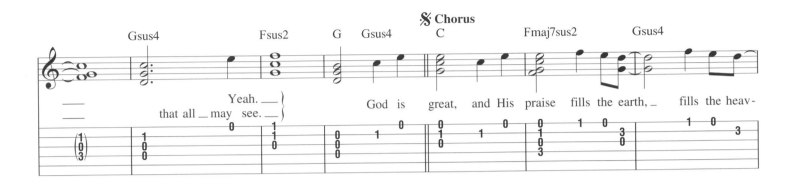

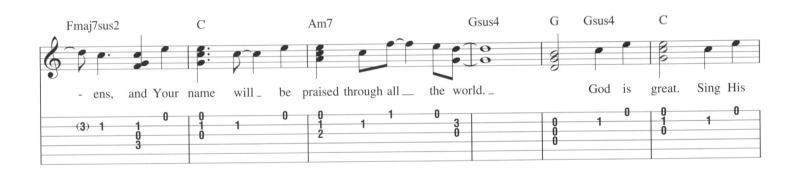

To Coda 1 ⊕

To Coda 2 ⊕

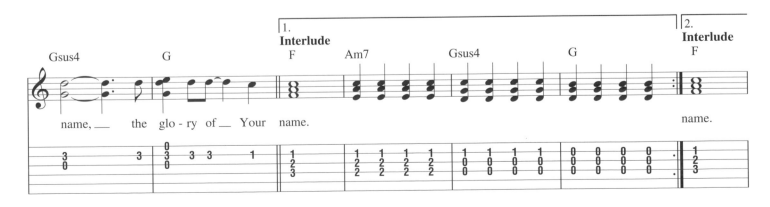

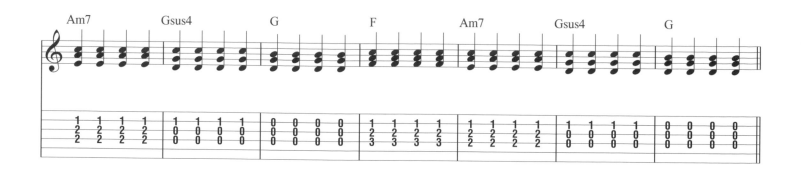

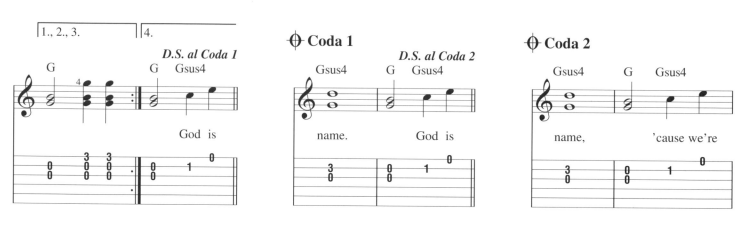

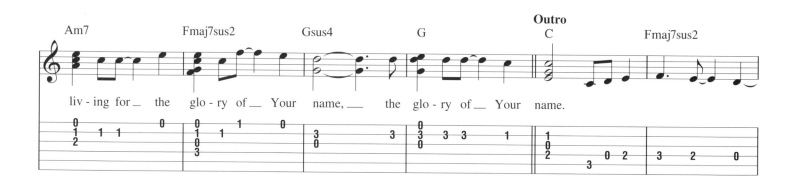

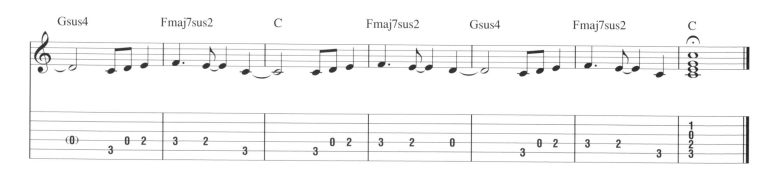

Lead Me to the Cross

Words and Music by Brooke Fraser

*Capo II

Strum Pattern: 3
Pick Pattern: 3

*Optional: To match recording, place capo at 2nd fret.

1. Sav-ior, I come, ___ qui-et my soul, ___ re-mem - ber ___
2. You were as I, ___ tempt-ed and tried, ___ hu - man. ___

re-demp-tion's hill ___ where Your blood was spilled ___ for my ran - som. ___
The Word be-came flesh, ___ bore my sin and death, ___ now You're ris - en. ___

Pre-Chorus

Ev-'ry-thing I once held dear, _ I count it all __ as loss. __ Lead me to the

*2nd time only.

Chorus

cross where Your love poured out. __ Bring me to my knees, Lord, I lay me down. _ Rid me of my-

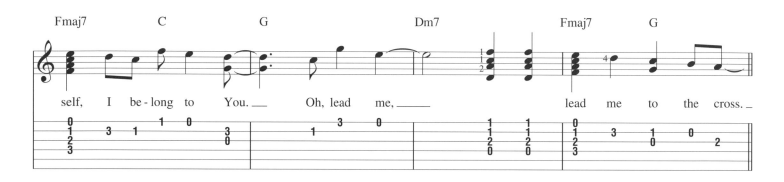

self, I be-long to You. __ Oh, lead me, _____ lead me to the cross.

Interlude

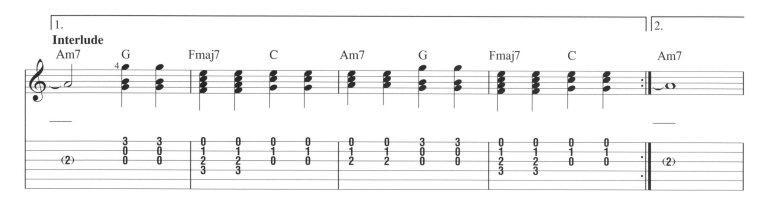

Bridge

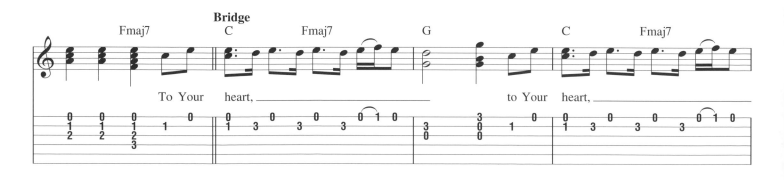

To Your heart, _____ to Your heart, _____

26

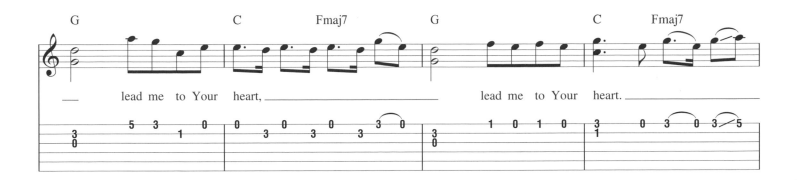

lead me to Your heart,_____ lead me to Your heart._____

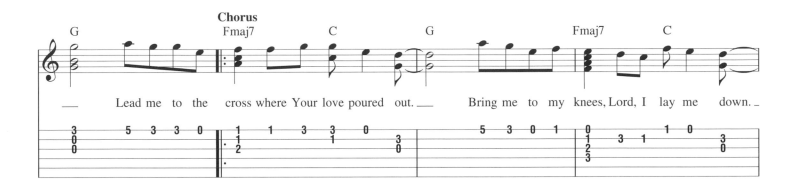

Chorus

Lead me to the cross where Your love poured out.___ Bring me to my knees, Lord, I lay me down.___

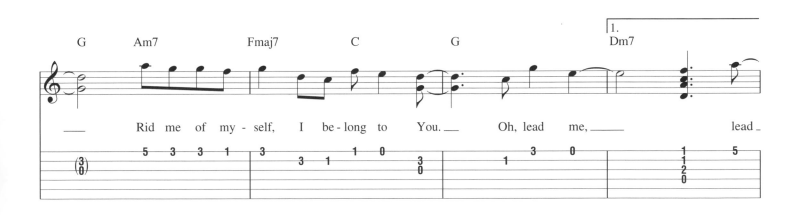

___ Rid me of my - self, I be - long to You.___ Oh, lead me,_____ lead ___

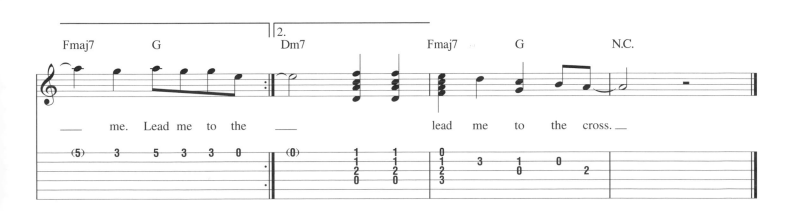

___ me. Lead me to the ___ lead me to the cross.___

Hosanna

Words and Music by Brooke Fraser

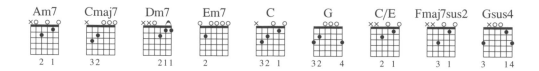

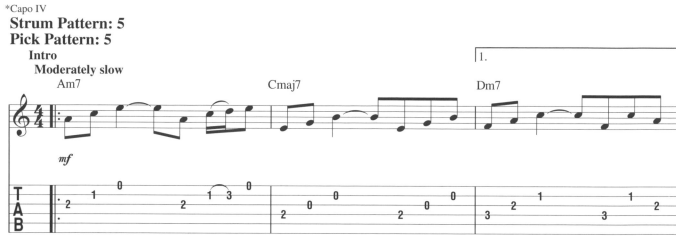

*Capo IV

Strum Pattern: 5
Pick Pattern: 5

Intro
Moderately slow

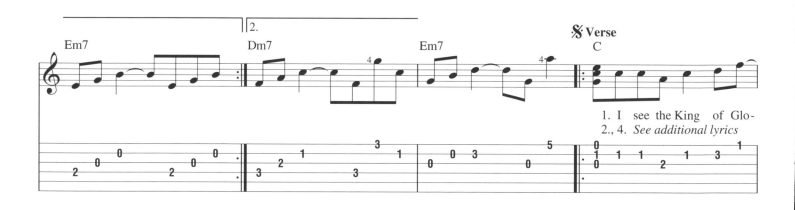

*Optional: To match recording, place capo at 4th fret.

1. I see the King of Glo-
2., 4. *See additional lyrics*

-ry ___ com-ing on the clouds with fire; ___ the whole earth shakes, the whole earth shakes, Yeah. ___

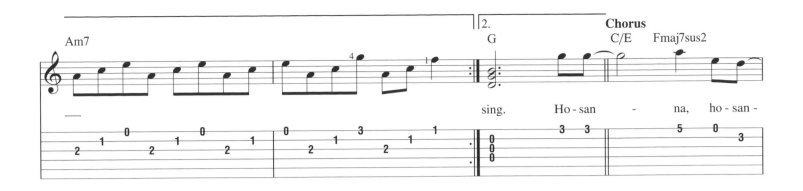

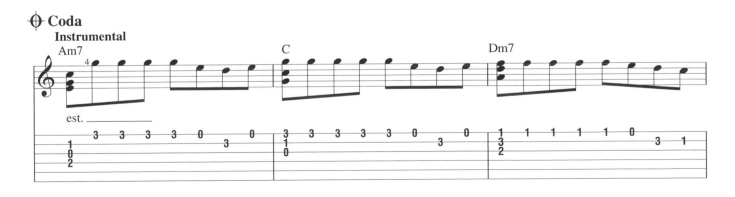

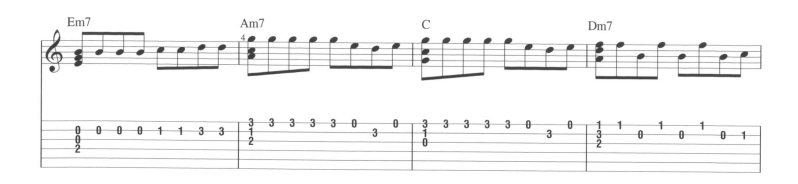

Bridge

Heal my heart and make it clean. _ O - pen up my eyes to the

things un - seen. _ Show me how to love _ like You _ have loved me.

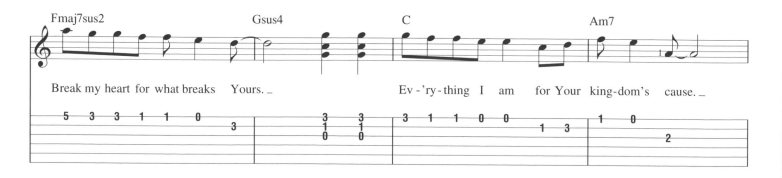

Break my heart for what breaks Yours. _ Ev - 'ry - thing I am for Your king - dom's cause. _

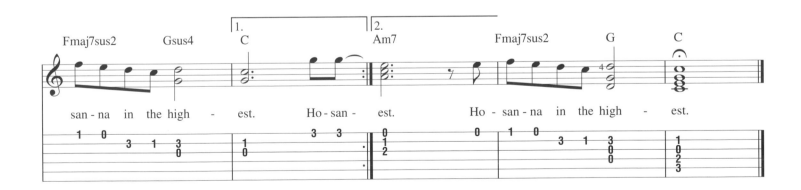

Additional Lyrics

2. I see His love and mercy
   Washing over all our sin;
   The people sing, the people sing.

4. I see a near revival
   Stirring as we pray and seek;
   We're on our knees, we're on our knees.

King of Majesty

Words and Music by Marty Sampson

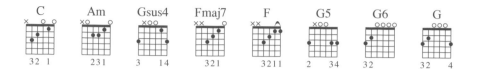

*Tune down 1/2 step:
(low to high) E♭-A♭-D♭-G♭-B♭-E♭

Strum Pattern: 6, 4
Pick Pattern: 1

*Optional: To match recording, tune down 1/2 step.

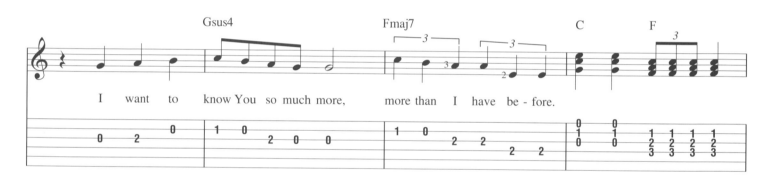

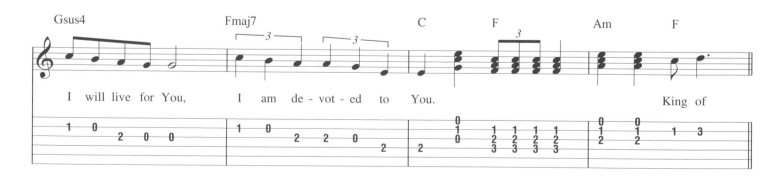

One Way

Words and Music by Joel Houston and Jonathon Douglass

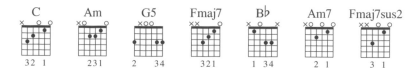

*Tune down 1/2 step:
(low to high) E♭-A♭-D♭-G♭-B♭-E♭

Strum Pattern: 1, 5
Pick Pattern: 3

Intro
Moderately

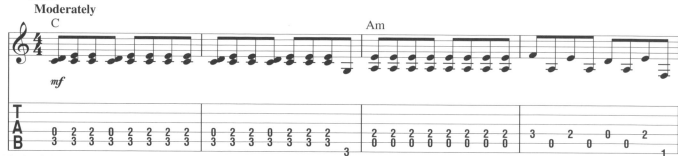

*Optional: To match recording, tune down 1/2 step.

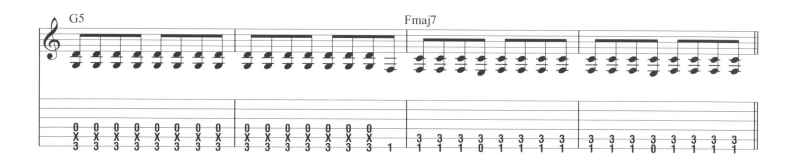

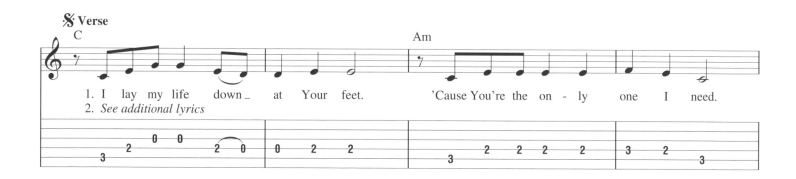

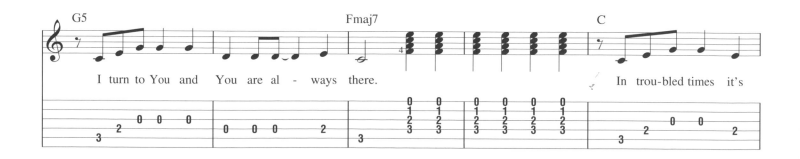

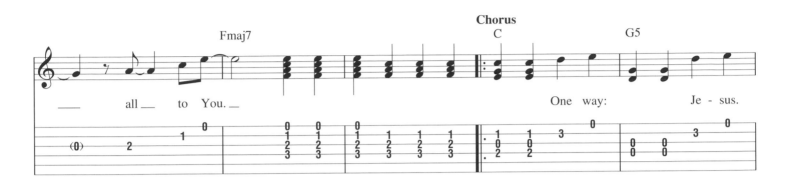

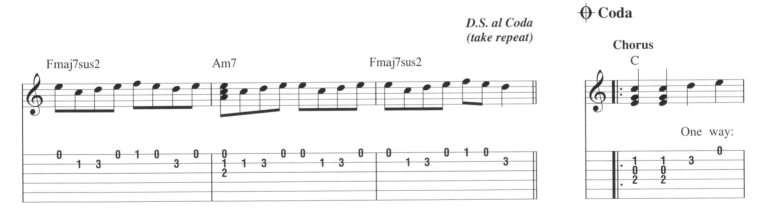

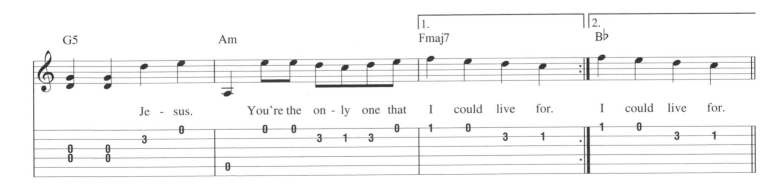

Bridge

You are the Way, the Truth and the Life. We live ___ by faith and not by sight for You. We're

*3rd & 4th times, sung one octave higher.

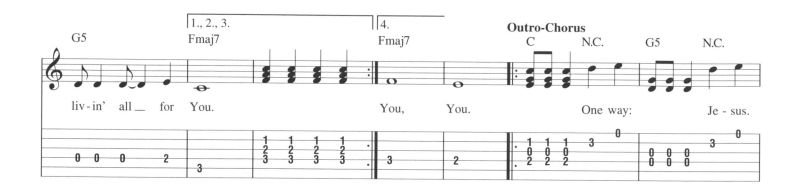

[1., 2., 3.] **[4.]** **Outro-Chorus**

liv-in' all ___ for You. You, You. One way: Je - sus.

[1.] **[2.]**

You're the on-ly one that I could live for. I could live for. One way: Je - sus.

[1.] **[2.]**

You're the on-ly one that I could live for. I could live for. ___

Additional Lyrics

2. You are always, always there,
   Every how and everywhere.
   Your Grace abounds so deeply within me.
   And You will never, ever change,
   Yesterday, today, the same.
   Forever 'til forever meets no end.

Shout Unto God

Words and Music by Joel Houston and Marty Sampson

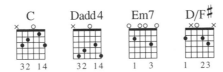

*Capo II

Strum Pattern: 1, 2
Pick Pattern: 2, 5

*Optional: To match recording, place capo at 2nd fret.

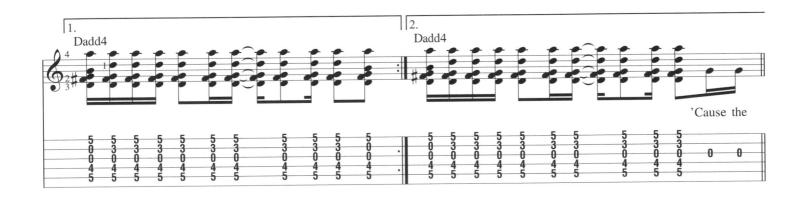

'Cause the

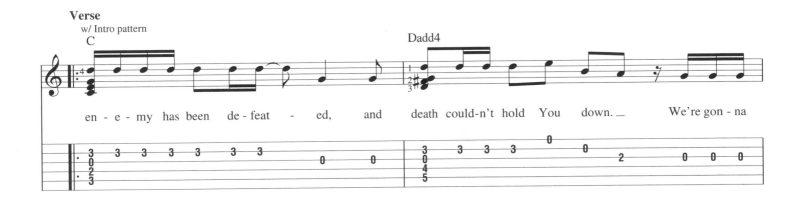

en - e - my has been de - feat - ed, and death could-n't hold You down. __ We're gon - na

lift our voice in vic - to - ry, we're gon - na make Your prais - es _____ loud. _ { 1. The / 2.-4. 'Cause the

en - e - my has been de - feat - ed, and death could-n't hold You down. _ We're gon - na
(Shout un - to God with a voice of tri - umph. Shout un - to God with a voice of praise.

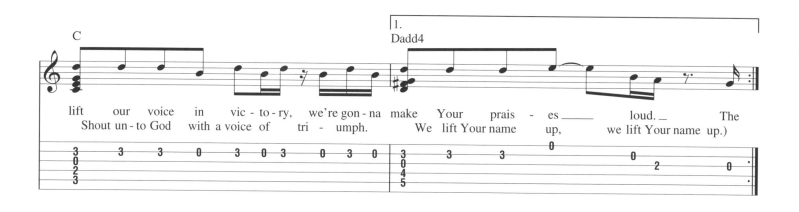

lift our voice in vic - to - ry, we're gon - na make Your prais - es _____ loud. _ The
Shout un - to God with a voice of tri - umph. We lift Your name up, we lift Your name up.)

make Your prais - es _____ loud. _ Shout un - to God with a voice of tri - umph.
We lift Your name up, we lift Your name up.)

*Let chord ring.

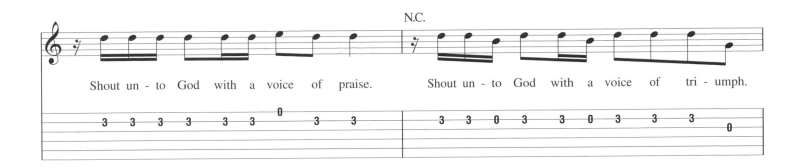

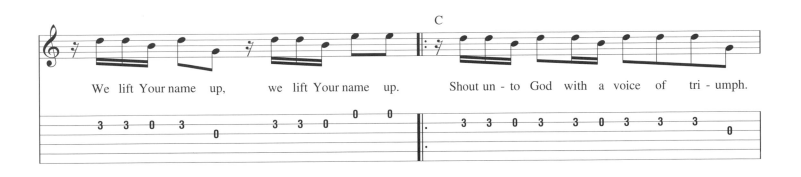

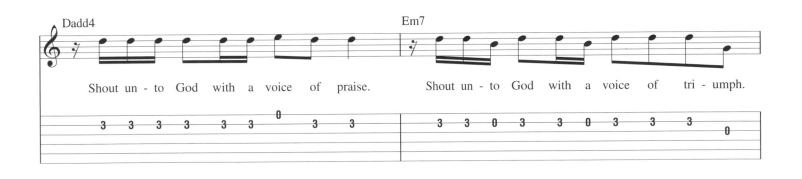

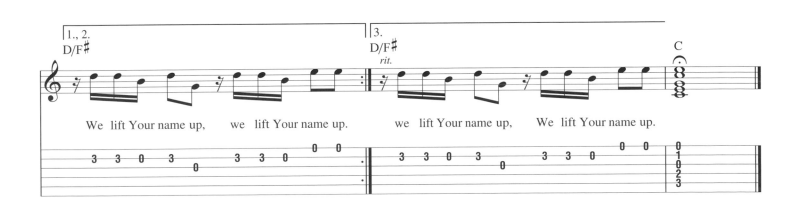

Salvation Is Here

Words and Music by Joel Houston

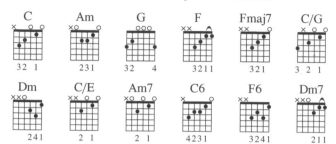

*Tune down 1/2 step:
(low to high) E♭-A♭-D♭-G♭-B♭-E♭

Strum Pattern: 1, 6
Pick Pattern: 2, 4

Intro
Moderate Rock

Verse

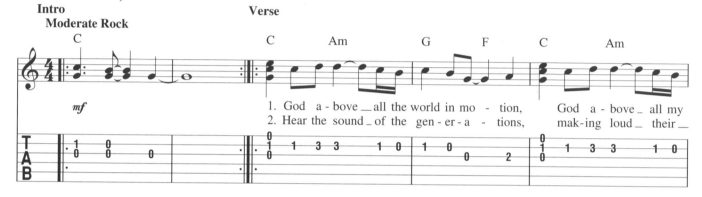

1. God a - bove __ all the world in mo - tion, God a - bove __ all my
2. Hear the sound __ of the gen - er - a - tions, mak - ing loud __ their __

hopes and fears. _____ And I don't care __ what the world throws at _____ me now. I'm gon-na
free - dom song, _____ all in all __ that the world would know __ Your name. We're gon-na

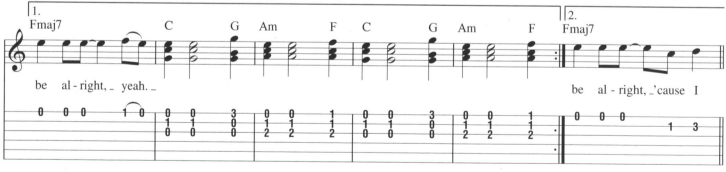

be al - right, _ yeah. __   be al - right, _'cause I

Chorus

know my __ God saved the day, _ and I know __ His __ Word nev - er fails, _ and I know _

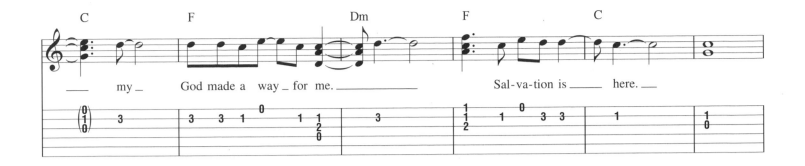

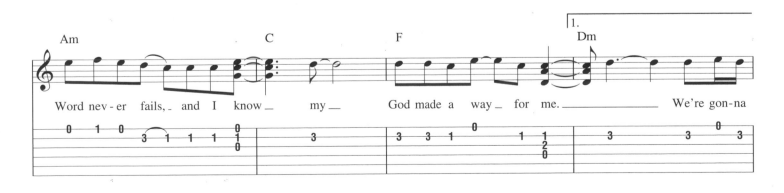

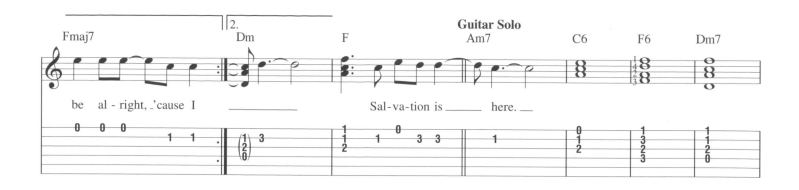

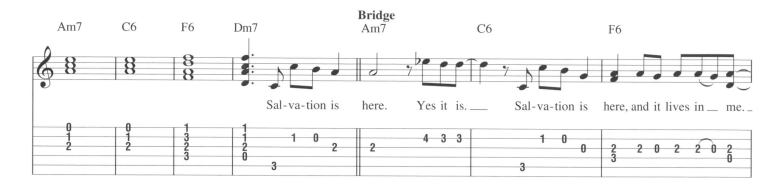

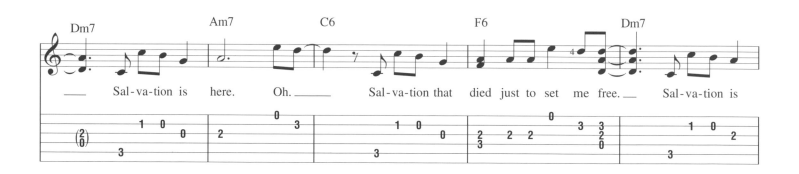

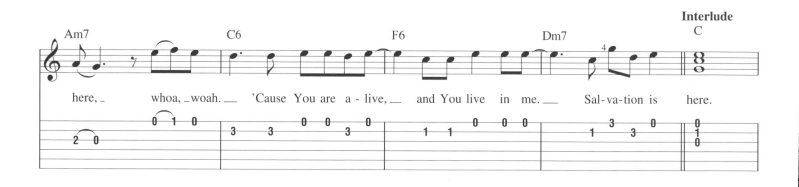

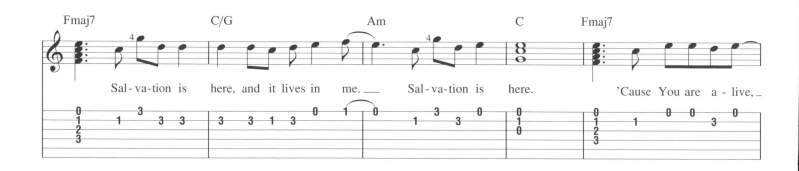

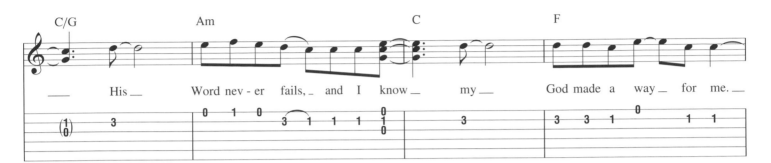

*1st time, let chords ring,
next 7 meas.

**1st time only.

Saviour King

Words and Music by Marty Sampson and Mia Fieldes

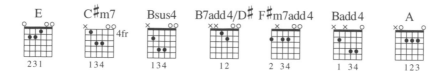

*Capo I

Strum Pattern: 2
Pick Pattern: 2

Intro
Moderately

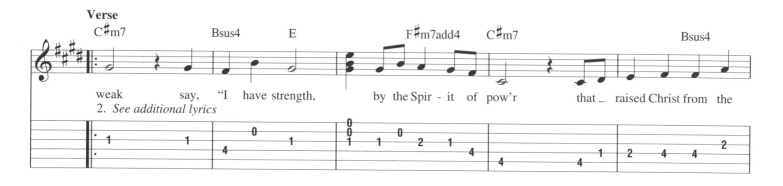

*Optional: To match recording place capo at 1st fret.

1. Let now the

Verse

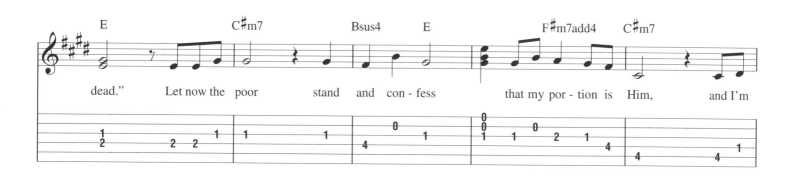

weak   say,   "I have strength,   by the Spir - it of pow'r   that _ raised Christ from the
2. *See additional lyrics*

dead."   Let now the poor   stand   and con - fess   that my por - tion is   Him,   and I'm

Pre-Chorus

more   than   blessed.   Let now our hearts burn with a flame,   a fire con-sum-ing all for

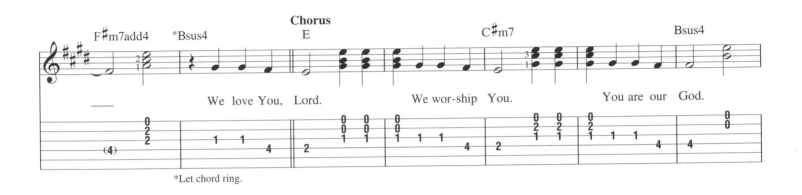

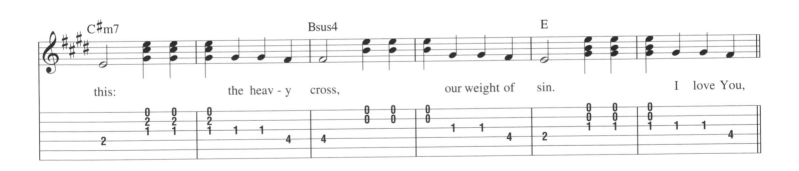

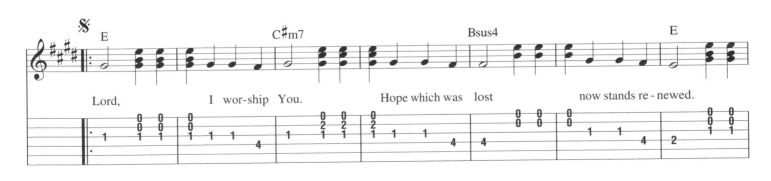

*Let chord ring.

Additional Lyrics

2. Let now Your church shine as the bride
   That You saw in Your heart as You offered up Your life.
   And now the lost be welcomed home by the saved and redeemed,
   Those adopted as Your own.

The Stand

Words and Music by Joel Houston

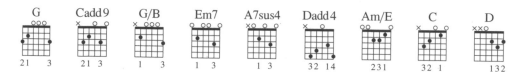

*Capo II

Strum Pattern: 3, 4
Pick Pattern: 2, 5

Verse
Moderately slow

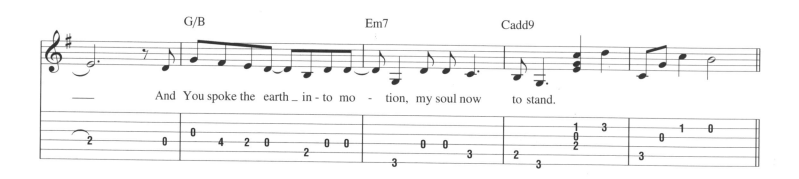

1. You stand be-fore _ cre-a-tion, e-ter-ni-ty in _ Your hands.

*To match recording, place capo at 2nd fret.

And You spoke the earth _ in-to mo-tion, my soul now to stand.

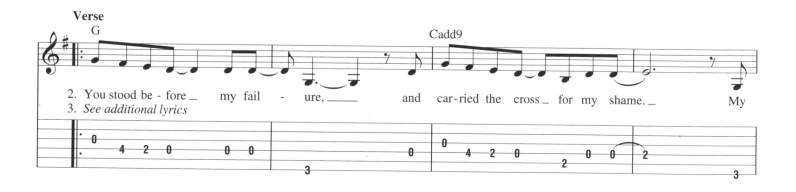

Verse

2. You stood be-fore _ my fail-ure, _ and car-ried the cross _ for my shame. _ My
3. *See additional lyrics*

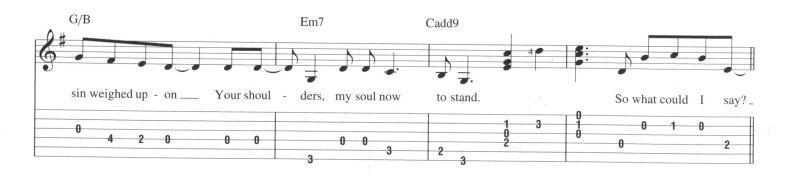

sin weighed up-on _ Your shoul-ders, my soul now to stand. So what could I say? _

*Let chord ring.

Additional Lyrics

3. So I'll walk upon salvation,
Your Spirit alive in me.
This life to declare Your promise,
My soul now to stand.

Take It All

Words and Music by Matt Crocker, Marty Sampson and Scott Ligertwood

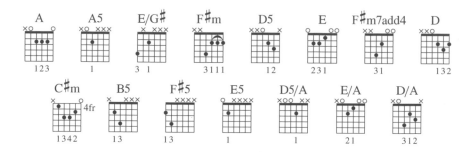

*Capo II

Strum Pattern: 1, 3
Pick Pattern: 1, 3

Intro
Moderately fast

*Optional: To match recording, place capo at 2nd fret.

**3rd time, sung one octave higher, next 5 1/2 meas.

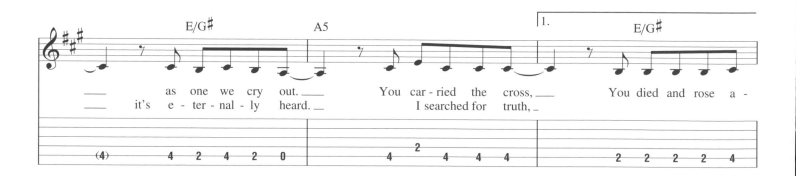

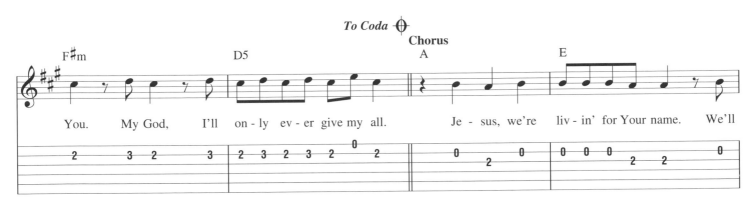

To Coda ⊕
Chorus

*Let chord ring.

Je - sus, we're liv- in' for Your name. We'll nev-er be a-shamed of You. _ Oh, whoa, oh, oh.

*Capo II

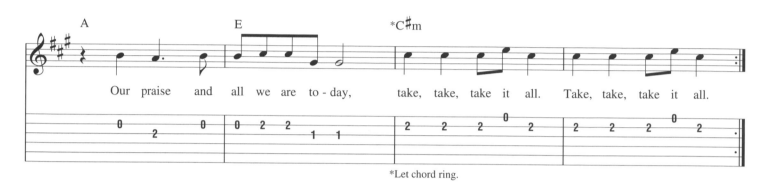

Our praise and all we are to - day, take, take, take it all. Take, take, take it all.

*Let chord ring.

Run- ning to the One who heals _

_ the blind, _ fol-low-ing the Shin - ing Light. _ In Your hands the pow'r to save _

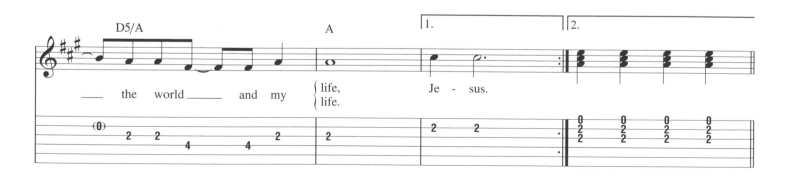

_ the world _ and my life, life. Je - sus.

Interlude

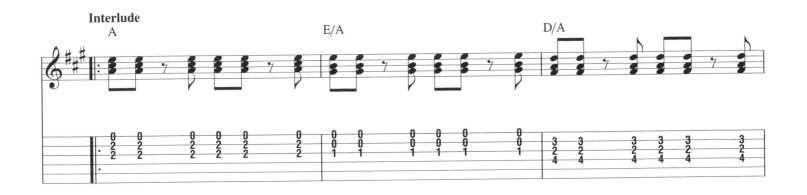

Outro-Chorus

*1st time, N.C., next 8 meas.

Je - sus, we're liv - in' for Your name. We'll

nev - er be a-shamed of You. __ Oh, whoa, oh, oh. Our praise and all we are to - day,

take, take, take it all. Take, take, take it all. Take take, take it all.

**Let chord ring.

Til I See You

Words and Music by Joel Houston and Jadwin Gillies

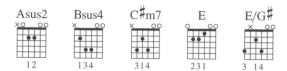

Strum Pattern: 3
Pick Pattern: 1

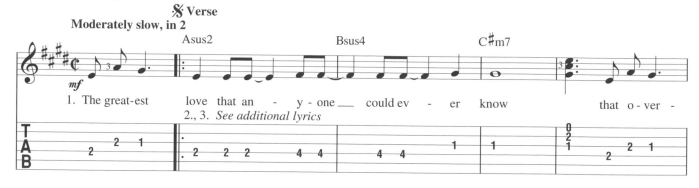

The Time Has Come

Words and Music by Joel Houston

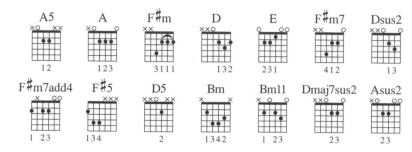

Strum Pattern: 1, 6
Pick Pattern: 1, 4

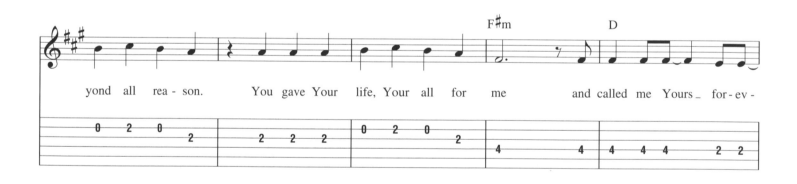

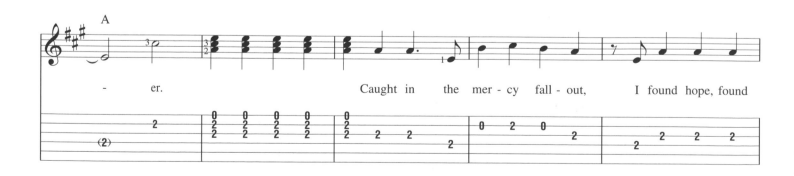

𝄋 Pre-Chorus

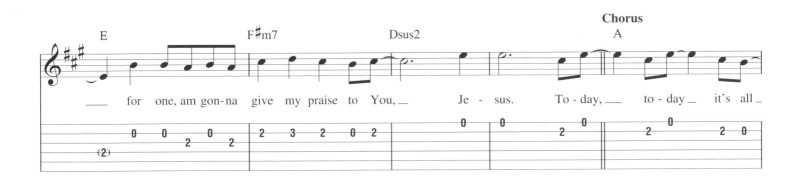

Chorus

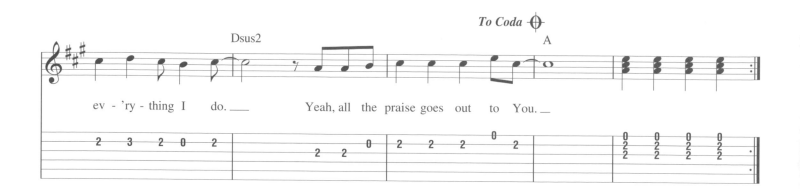

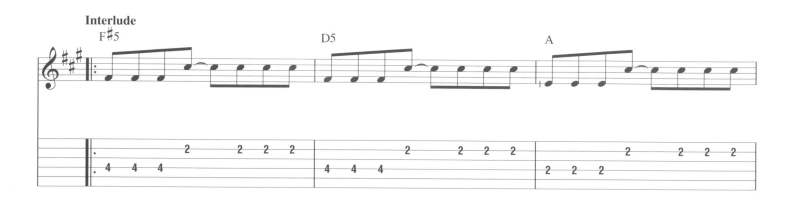

*Bass arr. for gtr., next 4 meas.

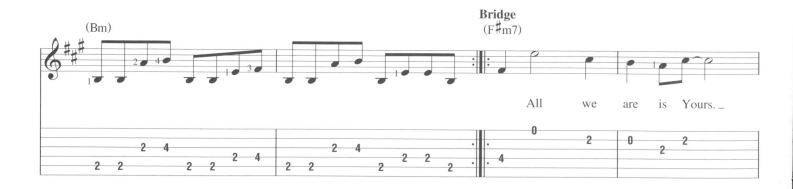

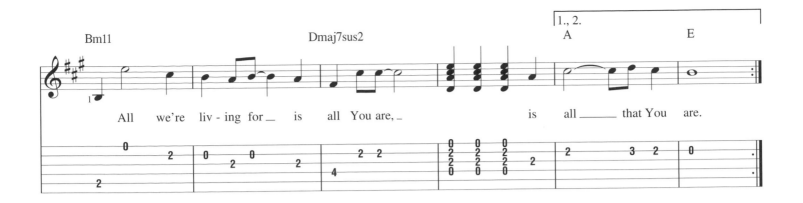

All we're liv-ing for __ is all You are, __ is all _____ that You are.

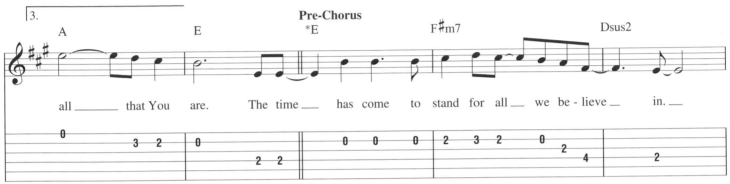

all _____ that You are. The time __ has come to stand for all __ we be-lieve __ in. __

*Let chords ring, next 8 meas.

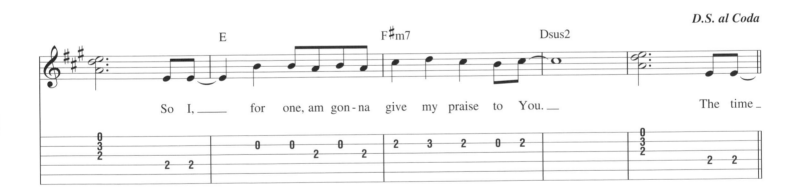

D.S. al Coda

So I, __ for one, am gon-na give my praise to You. __ The time _

Coda

In ev-'ry-thing I do, __ yeah, all the praise goes out to You. __

Tell the World

Words and Music by Marty Sampson, Joel Houston and Jonathon Douglass

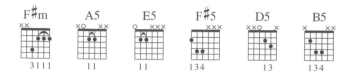

Strum Pattern: 1, 5
Pick Pattern: 1

Intro
Moderately

1. Don't wan-na stand here and shout Your praise and walk a-way and for-get
2. No long-er I, but Christ __ in me, __ 'cause it's the truth that set __

Your name.
__ me free. __

I'll stand for You if it's all I do
How could this world be a bet-ter place __

Pre-Chorus

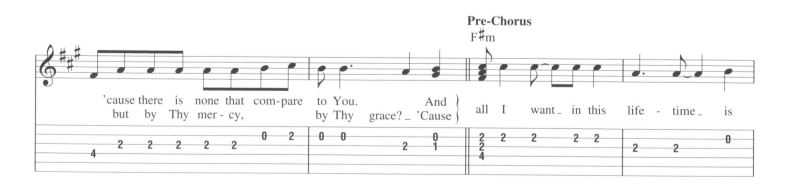

'cause there is none that com-pare to You. And
but by Thy mer-cy, by Thy grace? __ 'Cause

all I want __ in this life - time __ is

You. And all I want in this whole world is

To Coda 1 ⊕

Chorus

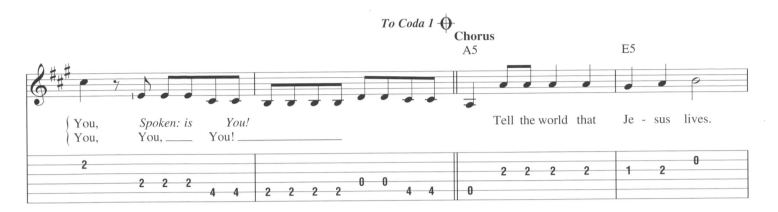

You, *Spoken: is* You!
You, You, You!

Tell the world that Je - sus lives.

Tell the world that, tell the world that. Tell the world that He died for them. Tell the world that He

⊕ **Coda 1**

D.C. al Coda 1
(no repeat)

𝄋 **Chorus**

lives a - gain.

Tell the world that Je - sus lives. Tell the world that,

4th time, To Coda 2 ⊕

tell the world that. Tell the world that He died for them. Tell the world that He lives a - gain.

Interlude

*1st time, N.C., next 8 meas.

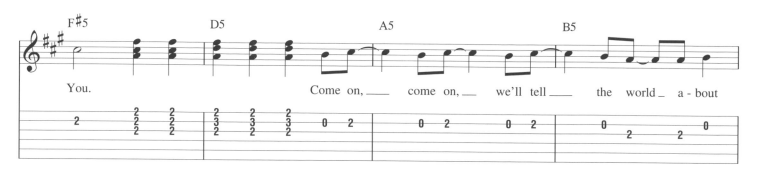

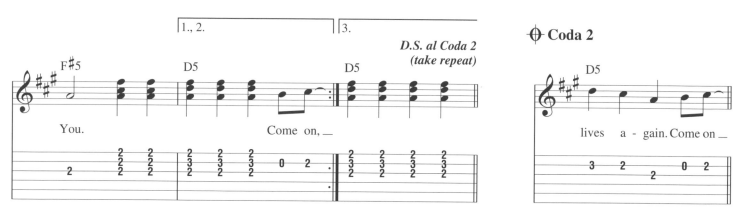

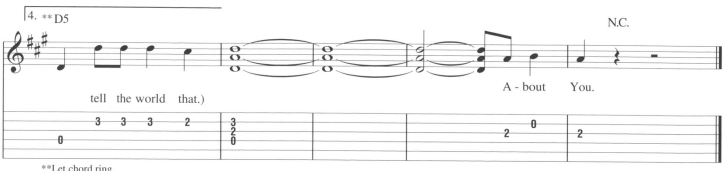

**Let chord ring.

christianguitarsongbooks

ACOUSTIC GUITAR WORSHIP

30 praise song favorites arranged for guitar, including: Awesome God • Forever • I Could Sing of Your Love Forever • Lord, Reign in Me • Open the Eyes of My Heart • and more.
00699672 Solo Guitar.. $9.95

BEST OF STEVEN CURTIS CHAPMAN

This revised edition features 15 songs from Steven's amazing career, including: All Things New • The Change • For the Sake of the Call • The Great Adventure • His Eyes • His Strength Is Perfect • Live Out Loud • Much of You • Speechless • and more.
00702033 Easy Guitar with Notes & Tab $14.95

CHRISTIAN ACOUSTIC FAVORITES

14 hits from some of the most popular names in contemporary Christian music, such as Switchfoot, Jeremy Camp, and David Crowder*Band. Songs include: All I Need • Dare You to Move • Holy Is the Lord • My Will • No Better Place • Open the Eyes of My Heart • What If • Wholly Yours • and more.
00702237 Easy Guitar with Notes & Tab $12.95

BEST OF CONTEMPORARY CHRISTIAN

Chords, strum patterns and lyrics for 20 CCM favorites in their original keys playable with movable chord types. Includes: Agnus Dei • Awesome God • Butterfly Kisses • El Shaddai • Father's Eyes • Friends • The Great Divide • I Could Sing of Your Love Forever • Jesus Freak • The Potter's Hand • more.
00699531 Strum It Guitar $12.95

CONTEMPORARY CHRISTIAN FAVORITES

20 great easy guitar arrangements of contemporary Christian songs, including: El Shaddai • Friends • He Is Able • I Will Be Here • In the Name of the Lord • In Christ Alone • Love in Any Language • Open My Heart • Say the Name • Thy Word • Via Dolorosa • and more.
00702006 Easy Guitar with Notes & Tab $9.95

FAVORITE HYMNS FOR EASY GUITAR

48 hymns, including: All Hail the Power of Jesus' Name • Amazing Grace • Be Thou My Vision • Blessed Assurance • Fairest Lord Jesus • I Love to Tell the Story • In the Garden • Let Us Break Bread Together • Rock of Ages • Were You There? • When I Survey the Wondrous Cross • and more.
00702041 Easy Guitar with Notes & Tab $9.95

GOSPEL FAVORITES FOR GUITAR

An amazing collection of 49 favorites, including: Amazing Grace • Did You Stop to Pray This Morning • How Great Thou Art • The King Is Coming • My God Is Real • Nearer, My God to Thee • The Old Rugged Cross • Precious Lord, Take My Hand • Will the Circle Be Unbroken • and more.
00699374 Easy Guitar with Notes & Tab $14.95

GOSPEL GUITAR SONGBOOK

Includes notes & tab for fingerpicking and Travis picking arrangements of 15 favorites: Amazing Grace • Blessed Assurance • Do Lord • I've Got Peace Like a River • Just a Closer Walk with Thee • O Happy Day • Precious Memories • Rock of Ages • Swing Low, Sweet Chariot • There Is Power in the Blood • When the Saints Go Marching In • and more!
00695372 Guitar with Notes & Tab $9.95

THE GOSPEL SONGS BOOK

A virtual bible of more than 100 songs of faith arranged for easy guitar! This collection includes: Amazing Grace • Blessed Assurance • Church in the Wildwood • His Eye Is on the Sparrow • I Love to Tell the Story • Just a Closer Walk with Thee • The Lily of the Valley • More Than Wonderful • The Old Rugged Cross • Rock of Ages • Shall We Gather at the River? • Turn Your Radio On • Will the Circle Be Unbroken • and more.
00702157 Easy Guitar $15.95

GREATEST HYMNS FOR GUITAR

48 hymns, including: Abide with Me • Amazing Grace • Be Still My Soul • Glory to His Name • In the Garden • and more.
00702116 Easy Guitar with Notes & Tab $8.95

HAWK NELSON – LETTERS TO THE PRESIDENT

All 14 songs from the debut album by these Christian punk rockers. Includes: California • From Underneath • Letters to the President • Recess • Right Here • First Time • Like a Racecar • Long and Lonely Road • Take Me • and more.
00690778 Guitar Recorded Versions............................ $19.95

from HAL•LEONARD®

THE HYMN BOOK

143 glorious hymns: Abide with Me • Be Thou My Vision • Come, Thou Fount of Every Blessing • Fairest Lord Jesus • Holy, Holy, Holy • Just a Closer Walk with Thee • Nearer, My God, to Thee • Rock of Ages • more. Perfect for church services, sing-alongs, bible camps and more!
00702142 Easy Guitar (no tab) $14.95

PRAISE AND WORSHIP FOR GUITAR

45 easy arrangements, including: As the Deer • Glorify Thy Name • He Is Exalted • Holy Ground • How Excellent Is Thy Name • Majesty • Thou Art Worthy • You Are My Hiding Place • more.
00702125 Easy Guitar with Notes & Tab $9.95

RELIENT K – MMHMM

14 transcriptions from the 2004 release by these Christian punk rockers. Features: Be My Escape • Let It All Out • Life After Death and Taxes • My Girl's Ex-Boyfriend • The One I'm Waiting For • When I Go Down • Which to Bury; Us or the Hatchet? • Who I Am Hates Who I've Been • and more.
00690779 Guitar Recorded Versions $19.95

SWITCHFOOT – THE BEAUTIFUL LETDOWN

All 11 songs in transcriptions with tab from the 2003 release by these Dove Award-winning alt CCM rockers: Adding to the Noise • Ammunition • Beautiful Letdown • Dare You to Move • Gone • Meant to Live • More Than Fine • On Fire • Redemption • This Is Your Life • 24.
00690767 Guitar Recorded Versions $19.95

TOP CHRISTIAN HITS

14 of today's hottest CCM hits: Blessed Be Your Name (Tree 63) • Dare You to Move (Switchfoot) • Filled with Your Glory (Starfield) • Gone (TOBYMAC) • Holy (Nichole Nordeman) • Holy Is the Lord (Chris Tomlin) • I Can Only Imagine (MercyMe) • Much of You (Steven Curtis Chapman) • and more.
00702217 Easy Guitar with Notes & Tab $12.95

TODAY'S CHRISTIAN ROCK

16 powerful contemporary Christian songs. Includes: Between You and Me (dc Talk) • Flood (Jars of Clay) • Kiss Me (Sixpence None the Richer) • Lord of the Dance (Steven Curtis Chapman) • Shine (Newsboys) • and more.
00702124 Easy Guitar with Notes & Tab $9.95

THE WORSHIP BOOK

Easy arrangements (no tab) of 80 great worship tunes, including: Above All • Days of Elijah • Forever • Here I Am to Worship • Mighty to Save • Open the Eyes of My Heart • Shout to the Lord • Sing to the King • We Fall Down • and more.
00702247 Easy Guitar.. $14.99

WORSHIP FAVORITES

21 songs: Above All • Ancient of Days • As the Deer • Breathe • Come, Now Is the Time to Worship • Draw Me Close • Firm Foundation • He Is Exalted • I Could Sing of Your Love Forever • Shout to the Lord • We Fall Down • You Alone • You Are My All in All • and more.
00702192 Easy Guitar with Notes & Tab $9.95

BEST OF WORSHIP TOGETHER

Includes 15 popular praise and worship songs: Forever • He Reigns • Here I Am to Worship • I Could Sing of Your Love Forever • Let Everything That Has Breath • more.
00702213 Easy Guitar with Notes & Tab $9.95

Prices, contents and availability subject to change without notice.

www.halleonard.com

0411